Original title:

Tropical Secrets

Copyright © 2025 Creative Arts Management OÜ

All rights reserved.

Author: Lucas Harrington

ISBN HARDBACK: 978-1-80581-640-9

ISBN PAPERBACK: 978-1-80581-167-1

ISBN EBOOK: 978-1-80581-640-9

Journey to the Heart of the Isles

A parrot squawks from a mango tree,
He's got gossip, oh so juicy!
Flip-flops slapping, what a sound,
As tourists stumble all around.

The sun smiles down with a playful grin,
While crabs in a line try to sneak in.
A local's laugh is loud and bright,
"Watch your drink, it might take flight!"

The Allure of the Misty Cove

Misty waves roll in with a wink,
As mermaids giggle over a drink.
Fish flex muscles, stealing the show,
While snorkelers wave, they scream, "Whoa!"

The hammock sways in a lazy breeze,
Belly flops sound with squeals and wheeze.
Local lizards dance in the sand,
Claiming, "We're the coolest band!"

Scent of the Hibiscus Hidden

Whispers float on the evening air,
With each step, be ready to bear.
A flower's scent, oh what a tease,
Follow it, if you please!

Lost flip-flops cause some dismay,
As seekers giggle on their way.
"Where's the path to paradise fun?"
"Just past the palm, under the sun!"

Reveries along the Glistening Coast

Beach balls bounce with a joyous cheer,
And sunburned folks hold cold beers near.
Seashells sing in a chorus loud,
While laughter gathers a colorful crowd.

Ice cream melts faster than a wink,
As kids try to conquer the drink.
"Surf's up, let's go!" they all shout,
But someone's lost their shorts, no doubt!

Sun-Kissed Secrets Beneath the Palms

Beneath the leaves, where monkeys grin,
A coconut fell and spun like a win.
Laughter echoes through warm, bright air,
As a toucan shouts, "Come dance if you dare!"

The sun beams down, with mischief in tow,
While flip-flops stumble, putting on a show.
A crab in a hat, what a sight to see,
Woos a shrimp with rhymes, oh so carefree!

Lush Canopies and Silent Vows

In thick green shade, the secrets thrive,
As giggling frogs in the marsh dive.
Whispers of love in a parrot's tune,
While fireflies blink beneath a laughing moon.

A sloth in a hat dreams of fame,
As a squirrel declares, "I'll win at this game!"
With murmurs of joy floating through the air,
Life's a wild ride with colorful flair!

Echoes of the Ocean's Heart

The waves tell tales of a fishy ballet,
As seagulls attempt to steal shells on display.
His fins made of glitter, a crab grins wide,
While a dolphin practices for the weekly slide.

A starfish crashes a shellfish party,
With dancing snails and snacks that are hearty.
Together they laugh at foolish old tides,
In the ocean's embrace, adventure abides!

Luminous Waters of Distant Shores

In waters that shimmer with giggles galore,
A mermaid sings songs of the sand's soft floor.
The jellyfish twirl with flamboyant grace,
While a crab steals the spotlight, it's quite the race!

Shells gossip tales of what swims around,
Oysters play poker on the soft seabed ground.
With humor afloat in the waves' playful churn,
Life in this haven is how we all yearn!

Starlit Confessions of Coastal Hills

Beneath the stars, the crabs did dance,
Whispering secrets in a lively prance.
The moon looked down, a mischievous grin,
As the waves giggled, inviting you in.

A parrot squawked a riddle or two,
While the lizards plotted a scheme anew.
The palm trees swayed with laughter so bright,
Sharing stories till the break of light.

A Parable of Lost Horizons

A clam in a shell, a wise old sage,
Tells of foolish fish on a watery stage.
The porpoise chuckles, a comedian grand,
As seagulls gossip about their next band.

With each wild wave, a new tale unfolds,
Of treasure chests and snails that are bold.
In this vast blue, where laughter runs free,
Even the starfish joins in with glee.

Melodies of the Hidden Lagoon

In a lagoon where the frogs sing sweet,
A turtle chimes in with a funky beat.
Fireflies twirl in a soft ballet,
While otters slide down to join the play.

With banana leaves acting as our stage,
Each critter laughing, escaping the cage.
They dance by the light of the glowing fish,
Making a wish, as dreams start to swish.

Legacy of the Sun-Kissed Reef

The fishes tease each other for fun,
As the coral glows in the warming sun.
A sea cucumber suddenly trips,
Causing a wave of giggly quips!

Jellyfish float with their whimsical flair,
Telling tales of their stylish hair.
The seaweed sways like a dancer's dress,
In the swish and swirl, we all feel blessed.

Veils of Mist Along the Shore

In the morning, clouds dance quick,
Seagulls squawk, they're quite the trick.
Waves like whispers, soft and light,
Tickle my toes, oh what a sight.

A crabs' ballad, quite absurd,
Claws clapping, playing the nerd.
Seashells gossip, telling tales,
While dolphins giggle in the gales.

Sunburned tourists, bright as pink,
Sunscreen splatters, and they wink.
Shuffleboard champions from afar,
Paddle ball kings, chasing the star.

With frozen drinks, our heads in whirl,
Sandy hats and bright string pearls.
A limbo contest, who will fall?
Laughter echoes, we've won it all.

Hues of Paradise Unveiled

Melons rolling down the hill,
Watermelons cause a thrill.
Mango madness in the air,
Watch out for the juice, oh dear!

Palms sway with a lazy wave,
Chasing coconuts is brave.
Cranky parrots squawk and shout,
Cheeky monkeys, in and out.

Bikinis bright, bold, and loud,
Mismatched patterns, stand out proud.
With flip-flops slapping on the sand,
Dancing like a road trip band.

From sunset hues to twilight sighs,
The fireflies mimic starry skies.
Life is a game, let's roll the dice,
In this realm, we smirk and spice.

Nectar of the Hibiscus Heart

Sipping juice from coconut shells,
Mango mustaches, oh what spells!
Limes in laughter, squeezed for fun,
Make life sweet like candy bun.

Dancing flowers swaying low,
Hummingbirds, oh what a show!
Fruit as vibrant as our cheer,
With every bite, joy draws near.

Pineapple hats worn askew,
Giggles as we sip our brew.
Banana slips on sandy ground,
Tumble down, laughter all around.

A feast awaits, a grand buffet,
Calypso beats lead the way.
In this paradise, life's a treat,
Hibiscus heart, can't be beat!

The Art of Island Solitude

On a chair, I find my bliss,
Shell phone ringing, oh what a miss!
Sunset brings a calming hue,
With wild thoughts of me and you.

A hammock swings, it creaks and groans,
My beach ball sings to coconut phones.
Gentle waves a soothing song,
Pina colada all day long.

Crabs parade in single file,
While I'm here in dreamer's style.
A flip flop toss, a jellyfish dive,
Island life, oh how we thrive.

Though seagulls steal my sandwich prize,
I chuckle up at their surprise.
In solitude, my heart will soar,
For laughter echoes, by the shore.

Fireflies Amidst the Palmetto

In the palms where shadows play,
Fireflies dance at the end of day.
One winks at me with a cheeky spark,
I swear it knows how to leave a mark.

They twirl in circles, a glowing parade,
While I ponder if I do look like a shade.
A swift mosquito buzzes by with glee,
Is it laughing at my attempt to flee?

With each bright flash, the giggles ensue,
Maybe they're plotting to prank me too.
I chase them down, but they're out of reach,
Guess I'll stick to the lessons they preach.

As the night thickens, the silliness grows,
Right under the moon, curiosity flows.
When fireflies giggle and share their flight,
I can't help but laugh at their bubbly delight.

Guardians of the Secret Cove

In a cove where waves meet the shore,
A crab in sunglasses is guarding the door.
He waves his claws like he's holding a sign,
"No fishing here, buddy! Just sip on some wine!"

Seagulls squawk, rehearsing their laughs,
As we dunk our toes in the saltwater baths.
A turtle passes with a wink and a grin,
Is he a lookout or letting us in?

The treasures they hold are buried in sand,
With ogling eyes, they make their grand stand.
A treasure chest spills, but it's all just shells,
And a rusty old spoon with a tale to tell.

In this secret cove, where humor flows free,
Laughter is currency, come swim with me!
We'll dance with the crabs, sing songs with the breeze,
And summon the tide with our giggles and ease.

Uncharted Paths of the Twilight Isles

On the paths where wild laughter roams,
We search for fruit that tastes like foam.
A map made of jelly beans and lies,
Leads us to snacks in disguise.

The parrots gossip with curious flair,
As we trip over roots and splatter our hair.
"This berry here? It's a delicacy!"
Or a booby trap set just for me.

Lemurs leap with a comedic flair,
They steal our lunches, not a single care.
In a chase that would make a movie great,
We find we've joined in a dance of fate.

As twilight paints the sky in jest,
We stumble on paths where we never rest.
Wrapped in giggles and wild delight,
We whisper to stars, "Let's dance through the night!"

Beneath the Warm Mists of Dusk

Beneath the mists where the odd things creep,
I heard the shadows giggling in their sleep.
Laughter drips from the leaves like dew,
Waking up shapes you never thought true.

A fox wears a hat, can you believe?
While shadows play cards, I'm left to weave.
With every glance, the silliness grows,
As the world reveals what nobody knows.

Silly frogs croak their top-secret tunes,
Inviting all critters to join 'neath the moons.
A charming parade of whims and cheer,
Here beneath the dusk, all's perfectly clear.

In the warm mists, as giggles ignite,
I join in the fun with sheer delight.
With whispers of wonder, I tiptoe around,
In a realm where the joy of strange laughter is found.

Chronicles of an Azure Horizon

In the land where coconuts sway,
The parrots dance in such a way.
They squawk and flap, quite the scene,
As they gossip 'bout the jellybean.

A crab in shades struts on the sand,
Looking for snacks, ain't life grand?
With every pinch, he steals the show,
And giggles as tourists say, "Oh no!"

The sun laughs loud with each bright ray,
Tickling waves that twist and sway.
While fish in socks play peek-a-boo,
As if they know a secret too.

A hammock swings, and so do heads,
As folks nap hard in their cozy beds.
Dreams of mermaids and ice cream cars,
Hide away under the laughing stars.

Secrets of the Sapphire Cove

Beneath the palms, the treasure lies,
But it's just old shoes and mango pies.
A map that leads to banana peels,
And treasure chests filled with silly squeals.

Crabs throw parties, wearing hats,
While dolphins join, and chat with bats.
The waves are music, quite a tune,
They dance along beneath the moon.

A pirate parrot steals a sock,
Hiding it away like it's a rock.
With every squawk, he claims a prize,
While fish roll eyes and swim in guise.

The tide comes in, the tide goes out,
Filling sponges with a happy shout.
Secrets linger where laughter flows,
In laughter's grip, anything goes.

Beneath Stars of an Ocean Dawn

Under a sky of sparkly dreams,
The jellyfish shine like moonbeam creams.
Starfish giggle as they sway and twirl,
While seaweed tangles in a whirl.

The turtles throw a morning toast,
To rise and shine, we love the coast.
With coffee brewed from seashell cups,
They cheer and sip, 'till morning ups.

A crab sings loud, though off the beat,
While pelicans dance on their big webbed feet.
The sun peeks in with rays of gold,
As fish trade stories, quite bold.

Starfish spell out jokes in the sand,
Creating laughter, oh so grand.
With every wave, a giggle flows,
As secrets hide where no one knows.

The Lore of the Seafarer's Soul

A sailor grins with a toothy smile,
He's been at sea for quite a while.
His map is marked with x's and y's,
But all he finds are coconut pies.

Mermaids laugh at his wild tales,
While ships get stuck in friendly gales.
Octopuses juggle with such delight,
While gulls spin stories in mid-flight.

In the crow's nest, there's disco night,
With pirate hats and garish lights.
The compass spins, the sea sings loud,
As the captain leads the merry crowd.

Every wave tells secrets anew,
In tides where laughter dances too.
For under sails, the world's a jest,
And it's the joy that trumps the quest.

The Heartbeat of the Palm Grove

In the shade where coconuts play,
Monkeys gossip all day,
Palm fronds wave with glee,
As if dancing near the sea.

Colorful birds sing out loud,
While the sun smiles, a golden shroud,
Laughter echoes, a silly breeze,
Whispers of mischief in the trees.

Crabs in tuxedos, all dressed fine,
Strut around like they own the line,
Shells like bow ties, so absurd,
A feast of giggles, it's not for the birds.

Under stars, the night falls cool,
Frogs croak jokes that break the rule,
In this grove, where fun is king,
Every critter has a song to sing.

Pearls Suspended in Time

Waves kiss shores with a bubbly grin,
Seashells laugh as they spin,
Glistening treasures buried in sand,
Echoing tales of a fanciful land.

Crabs wear pearls as their crown,
Drifting fish wear frowns upside down,
Mermaids giggle, just out of sight,
While dolphins dive, in pure delight.

A starfish winks, trying to be sly,
With starry tales that make you cry,
Time slips by in a playful trance,
As sea turtles join in a waltzing dance.

Coconut drinks under the sun,
Every sip is a cheeky pun,
In this paradise, a blissful mime,
Where laughter sparkles, suspended in time.

Transcendence of the Water's Edge

At sunrise, waves flap like a bird,
Whispers of fish, all quite absurd,
Sandy toes and sunburned backs,
With seagulls plotting sneaky snacks.

Jellyfish float with jelly in mind,
While octopuses try to unwind,
Sandcastles with quirky flags,
Each brick a story, with plenty of jags.

Starfish lounging like they own the place,
Silly crabs racing, a frantic race,
Turtles with sunglasses, oh so cool,
In this water playground, all are a fool.

As the sun dips down like a shy tease,
Laughter rings through the dancing breeze,
At the water's edge, joy does merge,
Where giggles and splashes begin to surge.

Essence of the Emerald Depths

Beneath the waves, a wacky spree,
Mermaids giggle, sipping their tea,
Seaweed swings like a funky band,
With fish in ties forming a grandstand.

Coral castles, in shimmering hues,
Host a party for all the blues,
Clams tell tales while octopus plays,
An underwater comic's crazy ways.

Amidst the bubbles, laughter erupts,
As turtles and fish bump like pups,
In this emerald realm of silly whims,
Every heartbeat dances on fins.

With whispers of tides, they bring delight,
In the depths where day meets night,
Laughter echoes in aquatic tang,
Where joy and mischief forever hang.

Riddles of the Sea's Embrace

A crab danced sideways near the shore,
With one big pinch, it knocked on a door.
The fish laughed loudly, swimming by,
They asked the shell: 'Hey, why so shy?'

Seagulls squawk in silly tones,
They play tag with the beach's bones.
A jellyfish wore a feathered hat,
While starfish giggle, 'Oh, what of that?'

The tide reveals secrets, oh so strange,
Like octopuses doing a courtly change.
With each wave, they laugh and tease,
In the sea's embrace, there's no time to freeze!

So come join this jolly, watery spree,
Where nothing's serious, just surf and glee.
The ocean's a stage, let's give a cheer,
For life in the splash is what we hold dear!

Fragments of a Coastline Dream

A coconut fell with a thud and a grin,
It rolled with joy, a playful spin.
The sandcastles laugh, 'We're here to stay!'
While crabs throw a party, hip-hip-hooray!

In the distance, a beach ball flies,
While mermaids giggle, don't be too shy.
Their tails glimmer in the sun's pure beam,
As they ponder if sand can dream a dream.

Seashells gossip under the sun's bright glow,
Telling tales of where the tide will flow.
With each scoop of sand, they plot and scheme,
Creating a world full of fun and cream!

Here where waves tickle the shore in delight,
Thoughts wander, taking a flight.
In this coastline adventure, laugh and play,
For each moment's a riddle, come what may!

Murmurs of the Glistening Waves

The surf whispers secrets to the shore,
As sea turtles waltz without a score.
Bubbles giggle, popping here and there,
While dolphins flip, showing off their flair!

A clam told a joke that went quite wrong,
Its friends all groaned, but they sang along.
The horizon stretches with laughter untold,
In this watery realm, craziness unfolds!

Waves chase each other with frothy grace,
While seaweeds wiggle in a silly race.
A floating pineapples starts to dance,
Inviting fish to join in the chance!

The moon smiles wide, as night begins to creep,
Insomniac stars can't help but leap.
In the laughter of night, waves softly play,
Sharing their tales until the break of day!

The Odyssey of the Forgotten Isle

On a sleepy isle, a parrot squawks,
Telling tales as the lazy sun walks.
With pirate hats and wooden swords,
The iguanas giggle, all bored with scores!

An old treasure map was found by a crab,
But it led to jellybeans—oh, what a fab!
The islanders chuckled, rolling on sand,
As gummy bears rained—a sweet, sticky band!

Under palm leaves where shadows stretch long,
Echoes of laughter blend with a song.
The breeze blows with whimsy, bright and absurd,
As turtles play chess, a laugh unheard.

With each sunset painting the skies in delight,
The forgotten isle shimmers through night.
In these shores of mirth, where giggles reside,
Adventure unfolds like a wacky tide!

Reverberations of Nature's Secrets

In the jungle, a monkey plays,
Swinging and tumbling, bright sunny rays.
He steals my snack, oh what a caper,
Laughs at me with the wildest caper.

The parrot squawks with glee and sass,
Teasing me as I watch the grass.
A sunbeam dances on my nose,
What a show this wild life throws!

The iguana gives me a sly look,
As if he's plotting in the nook.
Chirping crickets sing at night,
While fireflies flicker, what a sight!

The laughter echoes, nature's jest,
A symphony of joy, truly blessed.
With each new day, a face anew,
Nature's playground, full of view!

Enchanted Whispers from Beyond

The waves are giggling, can you hear?
They've secrets of sandcastles, my dear.
Crabs scuttle sideways, acting sly,
While the seagulls swoop down from the sky.

With every tide, a new tale spins,
Of mermaids vowing to make us grins.
They brush their hair with shells so fine,
While I just sit with my two cokes, divine.

The coconut laughs, rolling away,
As if it knows how I want to play.
The palm trees sway and dance around,
In nature's ball, joy is profound!

Suddenly a breeze, a gust of cheer,
Tickles my nose, brings the ocean near.
Life's absurd in this salty land,
With whispers of fun, all just as planned!

Conch Shell Secrets in the Breeze

A conch shell sits upon the shore,
Whispering tales of ocean's lore.
It tells of fish that dance and spin,
And crabs with hats who never win!

As I listen close, I can't help but grin,
For jokes of the sea, I hear within.
The jellyfish giggle, glowing bright,
Casting shadows that dance in the night.

The starfish, wise, gives me a wink,
As if to say, 'What do you think?'
Life's a beach, a wild delight,
Who knew shells could gossip at dusk's light?

So I gather my friends, a motley crew,
With laughter loud, we start anew.
As capers unfold upon the shore,
The secrets of shells echo evermore!

The Rhythm of the Forgotten Isles

In the distance, a drumbeat calls,
Echoes of laughter in jungle halls.
Dancing leaves and shimmying vines,
Even the frogs jump to wild rhymes.

A sloth joins in, oh so slow,
He sways like he's on a pop concert flow.
His friends come in with a cheeky grin,
A party of critters, let the fun begin!

The palm trees twist, the coconuts sway,
Who knew they'd dance in a quirky way?
The rhythm flows through the sandy ground,
In this lost paradise, joy is found.

We twirl and spin, no care or dread,
With a cake made of fruit and things said.
Under the stars, with giggles so bright,
The songs of the night, a sheer delight!

Secrets Hidden in the Sand

In the grains, a crab does dance,
Making waves in a clumsy prance.
Shells gossip softly, tales to share,
Of a beach ball's journey through salty air.

Footprints lead to a buried lie,
Where lost sunglasses quietly cry.
A bottle with a message bold,
"Help! I'm trapped under a mound of gold!"

Seagulls squawk and laugh with glee,
At the sunscreen that melted on the knee.
Flip-flops find a partner too,
In a game of hide and seek, who knew?

So dig in the sand, feel the cheer,
Every scoop brings a new souvenir.
With each wave that crashes back,
More secrets linger in the sun's warm track.

Beneath the Banyan's Watchful Eye

Beneath the branches, squirrels plot,
Stealing snacks that humans forgot.
A lizard dons a sun hat bright,
Claiming shade as his delight.

Monkeys swing with wild intent,
Creating chaos, their own event.
"Catch me if you can!" they tease,
As they scamper through the leafy trees.

A picnic basket in disarray,
With ants doing the cha-cha ballet.
Under the banyan, tales take flight,
Of daring deeds from morning to night.

With laughter echoing, the day unfolds,
New stories emerge, both wild and bold.
In the heart of green, mischief thrives,
As the jungle's humor keeps us alive.

Tales From the Tides of Time

The ocean whispers with a wink,
Crabs hold court with a glass of pink.
Starfish gossip about the moon,
While mermaids chuckle to a catchy tune.

Each wave a tale, each splash a joke,
Fish throwing parties, feeling bespoke.
A dolphin dives, then jumps so high,
To impress the gulls that pass by.

Old shells recall fond memories,
Of treasure maps in salty breeze.
At dawn, the seafoam draws a line,
Around secrets lost to time, divine.

So listen closely when tides curl,
As nature unfurls its funny whirl.
In every ripple, in every rhyme,
Lies a laughter hidden in time.

The Enigma of the Aqua Horizon

At dusk, the horizon wears a grin,
Reflecting mischief with a splashy spin.
Fishes dance like they're at a ball,
While octopuses juggle, having a ball.

A sailboat drifts with a crooked mast,
Chasing whispers of the ocean's past.
The sky blushes, waves go slap,
As seagulls plot their next mishap.

Shells are eavesdroppers, having fun,
As the tide tells jokes beneath the sun.
"Catch me if you dare!" they call,
In a game of tag that enthralls us all.

So here we stand, on sand so fine,
Lost in riddles, in playful design.
With every sunset, a chuckle's born,
In the laughter of waves, we're reborn.

Dances on the Edge of Twilight

Under the stars, a party sways,
Jellyfish jiggle in a dazzling haze.
Crabs in tuxedos, do the cha-cha,
Seagulls squawk, like they're from a drama.

Laughter bubbles like fizzy soda,
A penguin's moonwalk, a shocking moda.
Flamingos gossip, tail feathers high,
In this wild disco, birds soar and fly.

The ocean grins, it's quite a show,
Waves whisper secrets we don't know.
As night slips away, the sun gives a wink,
A party so wild, it makes fish rethink.

When dawn breaks, the light's a tease,
Crab cakes flip, and throw back the keys.
Twirling in laughter, they take a dive,
In the dance of a moment, they come alive.

Covert Oasis in the Sun's Embrace

Hidden beneath a palm's soft sway,
A lizard in shades makes quite the display.
Coconuts roll as if they can dance,
While locals giggle, not missing a chance.

Fish in sunglasses swim past with flair,
Chasing after a crab with a comb in its hair.
Mangoes throw parties, ripe and divine,
As parrots squawk jokes over cocktails of wine.

This secret retreat is a riot of glee,
Where turtles sing tunes from a nearby tree.
Each day is a dance, a game of charades,
As nature plays tricks through the leafy glades.

But watch for the monkeys, always a catch,
They'll steal your sunglasses, and make a mad dash!
In this oasis, laughter takes flight,
As the sun sets softly, bidding goodnight.

Echoes of the Saltwater Serenade

The waves crash with giggles, a chorus so sweet,
A dolphin's performance, quite the treat.
Seashells applaud with a delicate clap,
While starfish all cheer, in a jovial flap.

Mermaids gossip, flipping their hair,
Trading tall tales of a pirate affair.
Clams share secrets under the moon,
As jellyfish jive to a sparkly tune.

Octopus conducts with eight frantic arms,
While sea turtles groove, using their charms.
Coral reefs shimmer with sparkling laughs,
In this underwater world, where joy never wafts.

When at last the tides gently sigh,
The echoes of laughter linger nearby.
As waves recede, and night takes the stage,
The ocean still hums; a bubbling rage.

Memoirs of a Distant Paradise

In a land where flip-flops reign supreme,
A donkey on stilts lives out a dream.
Palm trees gossip in the warm, soft breeze,
While iguanas plot, with mischievous ease.

Breezes blow stories of laughter and glee,
As kites take flight, wild and carefree.
Under the sun, every day's a surprise,
With llamas in shades bringing giggling highs.

A squirrel in a hammock enjoys a fine book,
Next to a parrot who won't overlook.
The fruit stands chuckle, colorful sights,
As smoothies blend whispers on hot summer nights.

This distant haven of humor and play,
Will dance in your heart, come what may.
When stars come out and the stories unfurl,
Forever, they whisper the joy of this world.

Guardians of the Glistening Shore

On sandy steeds, they prance with glee,
Shells for armor, oh what a sight to see!
Crabs in sunglasses, blocking the sun,
Even the seagulls join in for fun.

They dance on the beach, leave footprints galore,
Pastel-colored flip-flops, who could want more?
A whale in flip-flops, what a bizarre scene,
Each wave a giggle, oh truly serene.

The lighthouse winks, it's caught in the jest,
Shellfish gather 'round, who's in for a fest?
With cocktails served by a wise old fish,
Who knew the seaside could grant such a wish?

In the end, they all laugh, a chorus of cheer,
Hiding their secrets, but never a fear.
The ocean might whisper, but it's always a show,
Guardians of joy, where the good times flow.

Echoes of the Whispering Waves

Bubbles giggle as they pop on the shore,
Waves tell secrets, who could ask for more?
A dolphin in sunglasses does flips, oh so grand,
While crabs do a shuffle, forming a band.

The seaweed whispers, "Come dance with me!"
"Just watch your step, don't trip!" they agree.
With flip-flop pals, they sway to the tune,
Sea stars tapping, 'neath the light of the moon.

Laughter echoes back from the depths of the blue,
A parrot named Chuck shouts, "Hey, how are you?"
He steals the seashells, with a cheeky grin,
The ocean's an actor and we're all in.

As the sun dips low, they share a grand tale,
About sandy pirates and a giant whale.
With echoes of laughter and waves soft and brave,
Tomorrow comes calling, the fun will not cave.

The Palettes of the Evening Sky

Brush strokes of orange paint the horizon wide,
While turtles in tutus dance with pride.
The sun takes a bow, with a wink, it's off,
Leaving behind a crab with a scoff.

The clouds wear hats, each one quite bizarre,
As fireflies flicker like tiny guitars.
The breeze strums a tune from the evening's edge,
While pelicans gossip, oh what a pledge!

Stars pop like popcorn, scattered and bright,
A jellyfish hoedown in the soft moonlight.
Each sparkle a giggle, each twinkle a cheer,
In this canvas of night, nothing is drear.

As the colors fade, they promise return,
With more tales and giggles, the tide will churn.
In the cloak of the night, they frolic and play,
Guardians of laughter, come what may.

Folktales on the Breeze

Whispers ride high on the wind's gentle arms,
Where whispers of fish tell tales with charms.
A crab with a monocle spins grand old lore,
Of treasure maps hidden behind the coral door.

The parrots squawk loud, "Hear the news of the sea!"
"Got a joke for you, chuckle, let it be!"
With a wink and a nod, the barnacles grin,
Sharing tall tales with a splash and a spin.

Through laughter and giggles, the sea gets a glow,
As the wind carries secrets where only it knows.
Mermaids pull pranks with a flick of their tails,
While sea cucumbers tell of their epic fails.

The stars now listen to legends they weave,
Of a beach party night no one could believe.
From the depths of the ocean, the stories ascend,
Folktales on the breeze, where fun has no end.

Secrets of the Sun-Kissed Shoreline

On the beach, crabs dance around,
Building castles without a sound.
Seagulls squawk, plotting their joke,
Stealing snacks from a chunky bloke.

Sandcastles rise, then start to lean,
Towers tumble, it's quite a scene.
The sun shines bright, wearing shades too,
Even the sunburn laughs at you!

Footprints lead to nowhere fast,
Waves chase after the ocean's cast.
With each splash, a giggle's born,
As flip-flops fly and swimsuits torn.

So let the laughter fill the air,
Where the salty breeze plays with your hair.
At sun-kissed shores, secrets unwind,
In this sandy playground, joy you'll find.

The Language of the Rustling Leaves

Whispers swirl in the leafy green,
Trees gossip like you've never seen.
Squirrels pause mid-chatter, then dash,
While dandelions plot a funny clash.

A parrot laughs at a jogger's trip,
He seems to judge with every flip.
Leaves rustle secrets of wiggly bugs,
While ants throw parties, sharing hugs.

The wind starts singing a playful tune,
Dancing with flowers, a merry swoon.
Bushes chuckle, inviting a glance,
As daisies, with glee, begin to prance.

Nature's theater, an endless show,
Where laughter bubbles and breezes blow.
Listen closely, if you dare,
For the trees know jokes beyond compare.

A Tapestry of Sunset Dreams

The sky turns orange, a painter's thrill,
As clouds gather for a night-time spill.
Crickets tune up, a concert awaits,
While fireflies beam in glowing states.

The horizon grins, a cheeky smirk,
As surfers wipe out, it's quite the quirk.
A dolphin pops up with a splashy wink,
While kids build forts made of sand and pink.

Each sunset spills laughter like wine,
Reflecting joy in a dance divine.
Stars peek out, a giggling cheer,
The moon whispers secrets for all to hear.

As colors fade, the fun's not done,
With starlit skies, the wonders run.
In each twinkle, a chuckle bright,
Painting dreams across the night.

Moonlight over the Sapphire Sea

The moon spills silver on waves that sway,
As fish come out to join the play.
A crab holds court, wearing a crown,
While jellyfish float in a gown of brown.

Bubbles giggle, bursting with glee,
Telling tales of fish who flee.
The water winks, a playful tease,
While starfish flip and say, 'Oh please!'

Sailboats sway like kids in a dream,
As sailors sing of ice cream cream.
Seashells join in, creating a beat,
With echoes of laughter so sweet, so sweet.

Under the moon's bright, watchful eye,
Creatures dance as time slips by.
Each wave whispers joy, a soothing beep,
In this sapphire realm, our hearts take a leap.

The Secret Lives of Ocean Tides

The waves collect their salt and light,
Waltzing with the moon each night.
They giggle as they kiss the sand,
In a dance that's never planned.

Fish gossip in their underwater lanes,
While crabs plot out their silly games.
Surfers ride their slippery backs,
Laughing as the ocean cracks.

Seagulls sing of hidden treasure,
Belly-flops bring them all such pleasure.
Each splash a new tale to unfold,
In sea-spray stories echoing bold.

The tides always know when to tease,
Playing tricks, such playful ease.
They whisper secrets in salty tones,
With each splash, the laughter groans.

Rhythms of Nature's Palette

In colors bright, the hues collide,
Nature paints where secrets hide.
A parrot's squawk brings laughter near,
Each brushstroke tickles every ear.

The monkeys swing with such delight,
Playing pranks from morning light.
A coconut falls with a thud,
Sending giggles in the mud.

Breezes swirl with fragrant cheer,
Tickling noses far and near.
A canvas stretched on endless seas,
Nature's humor flows with ease.

Through laughter, colors boldly gleam,
As sunlight dances like a dream.
In this palette, joy's unleashed,
The world's a joke, how sweetly teased.

Whispers of the Island Breeze

The breeze carries tales of a funny kind,
Tickling leaves, leaving no clue behind.
With every gust, secrets are spun,
As palm trees sway, oh what fun!

It whispers to the sun-kissed shore,
"Hey, don't you remember the crab from before?"
Laughter echoes in the waves,
Where playful spirits dance and rave.

Turtles giggle at the sloth's slow pace,
While butterflies float in a dizzy chase.
The wind's a jokester, forever free,
Chasing shadows beneath the trees.

It wraps you tight in its gentle embrace,
Reminding you life's a merry race.
With whispers light as marshmallow fluff,
The island breeze says, "You've got enough!"

Hidden Gems of the Coral Coast

Beneath the waves, the colors play,
Coral castles in a splashy ballet.
Clownfish giggle, hiding their glee,
As shrimps tap dance for you and me.

Sea turtles slide by, calm and wise,
While octopuses hide in disguise.
The starfish hold hands in a circle of fun,
Join in the laughter, oh, don't be shun!

Jellyfish waltz with a graceful glow,
Their translucent beauty just steals the show.
"Why did the crab cross the bay?" they ask,
"To find a good home, simple task!"

The coral coast holds stories untold,
Of treasures found, and secrets bold.
In this underwater comedy scene,
The ocean's the limelight, life's a routine!

Echoes Beneath the Island Sky

In the shade of the palm, a crab wears a hat,
He dances 'round shells, a comedic little brat.
With every quick sidestep, the sunlight will glare,
The fish laugh aloud, brushing salt in their hair.

A parrot squawks jokes, perched high on a tree,
Squabbling with monkeys, 'Who's funnier, me?'
They throw their ripe bananas, quite a fruity assault,
While tourists just chuckle and chalk it up to fault.

The waves roll in whispers, the tide plays a trick,
Casting seaweed wigs on unsuspecting prick.
A turtle stops short—what's this on his shell?
"An aquatic Marcel," he chuckles; oh well!

Even the sunsets erupt in a laugh,
Painting the sky like a child's wild craft.
As night falls like curtains, the stars twinkle bright,
With giggles still echoing, all through the night.

Secrets of the Serene Breeze

There's a breeze blowing softly, with secrets to share,
It tickles the toes of a local fair hare.
This funny old bunny burrows in jokes,
While the sand crabs retort, engaging in hoax.

A smooth coconut holds tales full of glee,
"Have you heard what the shells did down by the sea?"
The pelicans chuckle, swooping down low,
"It's a comedy special! Come see the show!"

Laughter bounces off waves in a playful spree,
As the dolphins flip tricks, skipping with glee.
A sea turtle shakes, not quite sure how to dance,
With flippers a-flopping, he gives it a chance!

In the still of the night, the crickets sing clear,
With melodies cheeky that tickle the ear.
So gather 'round nature, embrace every jest,
In this paradise of laughter, you're bound to feel blessed.

The Coral Reef's Lullaby

The coral sings sweetly, a lullaby bright,
To fish in pajamas, who sleep through the night.
They snore like old pirates, a symphony grand,
While seaweed wriggles, it's just like a band!

A clownfish glances, "Great dreams I beseech!"
"Where's the last treasure? Just beyond the beach!"
With a wink and a nudge, the starfish reply,
In the deep of the reef, gold doubloons are shy.

A lobster in glasses, so wise and so sage,
Reads all the fish gossip, flipping the page.
"Who knew that sea foam could giggle and laugh?"
As an octopus blushes, it's overly daft.

When the sun starts to set, all creatures unite,
Sharing tall tales, a carnival night.
With sketches of rainbows, they'll paint the sea floor,
Where laughter and dreams will forever explore.

Beneath the Banyan's Embrace

Underneath the banyan, the stories unfold,
Of squirrels in sunglasses, getting too bold.
They scramble and dash, on the branches they race,
While birds drop their snacks, in a feathery chase.

"Catch me if you can!" cries a cheeky old lizard,
While daring the breeze, thinking he's quite the wizard.
The toads sit in clusters, all laughing quite loud,
"I'll leap the highest!" makes the audience proud.

Amidst all this chaos, a wise old owl sighs,
"My jokes from the tree tops are good, no surprise!"
The sunbeam breaks through, igniting the show,
As shadows dance wildly, putting on quite the glow.

Underneath the banyan, life seems a delight,
With giggles and grins, the moon hits the night.
For in every whisper and chuckle you trace,
Are the joyful confessions of this lively place.

Aromas of the Island Afternoon

The breeze carries scents of ripe guava,
Whiffs of coconut clash with my grandma.
She says to avoid the fruit so funky,
But it's just her way to tease the monkey.

Some pineapples dance in a hula show,
Wiggling their leaves like a wild burlesque flow.
Laughter erupts with a splash and a cheer,
A piña colada slides down like a spear.

Coconuts roll while the sun starts to beam,
A game of dodgeball, or so it would seem.
But the only threat is a seagull named Pete,
He'll steal your hat and dance off on his feet.

So let's savor the joy, sip drinks in the haze,
In an island afternoon filled with funny plays.
With aromas that tickle and stories that gleam,
It's all just a part of this silly sunbeam.

Colors of a Hidden Horizon

The sunset spills colors, a wild paint fight,
Crayons run rampant, oh what a sight!
Fuchsia and teal like a parrot on glue,
Bright oranges giggle, they don't have a clue.

In the distance, a kite-strangled fish,
Winks at me, making a rather bold wish.
"Catch me, I'm tasty, or maybe just fried,"
Said the fish with a laugh, swimming off wide.

Mangoes in hats stroll past proudly grinning,
Each fruit a contender, the contest just beginning.
With cherries as judges, the rules are pure play,
Who knew this paradise would brighten my day?

So here in this chaos, I'm feeling so bold,
With laughter and colors that never grow old.
The horizon is wild, like a carnival fair,
Where the fun bounces high, floating loose in the air.

That Which the Ocean Keeps

The ocean's a magician, a splashy old friend,
With treasures it holds that twist and they bend.
A flip-flop, a bottle, a sardine that sings,
Undersea conch shells with golden fish wings.

The waves giggle wildly, tickling my toes,
As mermaids practice their cartwheel throws.
Crabs wear their shells like a hat for a party,
Dancing in sand, looking cute and quite hearty.

A toothbrush floats by, on a quest for a smile,
While starfish plot world peace, in their own style.
The ocean decides on a playful surprise,
Waves thump like drums 'neath the tropical skies.

So watch what you toss in the shimmering blue,
For the ocean is known to keep things askew.
It's a kingdom of laughter, where joy holds the key,
And what it collects brings delight to the sea.

A Symphony of Shadows and Light

The palm trees sway to a rhythm so sweet,
As shadows tap dance on the warm sandy beat.
Light plays the maracas, while giggles hum tunes,
Making music with crickets, and laughing raccoons.

A pineapple sings in a jazzy old style,
With coconuts grooving, they dance for a while.
Their funky old moves make the sun laugh aloud,
While the clouds throw confetti, a fluffy white crowd.

The ocean joins in, rhythm clapping its waves,
Creating a symphony, perfect for knaves.
With all this commotion, not a frown in sight,
Who knew such a chaos could feel so polite?

So dance, you dear sunbeams, in shadows' soft grace,
In this silly concert, find your happy place.
A lively performance, through daybreak and night,
In a world full of humor, shadows, and light.

Enchanted Groves and Shadowed Paths

In groves where monkeys prance and swing,
A squirrel shouts, 'I'm king, I'm king!'
The parrots chatter, oh what a show,
As a turtle slides, moving rather slow.

Under palm trees, shadows dance light,
A lizard slips away, a comical sight.
Banana peels roll with a slippery fate,
While toucans laugh at the late-night date.

The path winds on with giggles abound,
As we chase a frog that leaps all around.
In this wild world, with laughter so loud,
We're all just jesters in a nature crowd.

With every rustle, there's fun in store,
A secret revealed, then one more encore.
So come, take a stroll through this whimsical maze,
Where foolishness reigns and the sun always plays.

The Serengeti of Cascading Vines

In the jungle where vines twist and crawl,
A monkey swings by, oh what a fall!
He lands with a thump on a soft leafy bed,
And giggles arise, filling up his head.

A parrot squawks loud, calling friends on the scene,
While a tortoise frowns, just trying to glean.
'No hurry!' he sighs, 'I'm just taking my time,'
As the chattering crowd breaks out into rhyme.

The chameleons flaunt colors bright as a flame,
Each shift in the hue is a hilarious game.
While vines, thick with laughter, hang low from the trees,

We sway to the rhythm of a cheeky breeze.

In this verdant theater, where whimsy takes flight,
Every twist holds a tale that is pure delight.
So come swipe your worries on this splendid retreat,
And join in the fun, life's a wild beat!

Whispers from the Ocean's Heart

Down by the shore, where secrets abound,
A crab dances sideways, slight and round.
With a flip of its claw, it beckons you near,
'Join in the fun, there's nothing to fear!'

The waves scoff and chuckle, then waltz on the sand,
As a seagull squawks jokes, oh isn't it grand?
A starfish plays shy, hiding in its shell,
While a fish in the tide is casting a spell.

A sandcastle rises with a crooked old tower,
Its royal occupants claiming their power.
But alas! A big wave comes crashing on through,
And all of them giggle, 'We were never meant to!'

So gather your joy, let the tide lift your soul,
In this playful realm, where laughter's the goal.
The ocean's heart whispers secrets and cheer,
In the rhythm of waves, your worries disappear.

Fables of the Breeze and the Beach

On shores of laughter, where stories are spun,
The breeze teases grains, oh what fun!
Seagulls swoop down, with cheeky delight,
While shells gossip tales of the day and the night.

The sun grins wide, casting shadows that prance,
As beach balls take flight in a whimsical dance.
A kid in a bucket stumbles with pride,
'Look at my castle!' in puddles they slide.

Waves whisper softly, 'Come, join in the cheer,'
While a crab yells back, 'I've got nothing to fear!'
With pails and with shovels, we build dreams anew,
On this sandy stage, the world feels askew.

So gather your giggles, let the salty air brim,
In this realm of fun, we're bound to the whim.
From breezy beginnings to the close of the day,
Life's a light-hearted tale, come along for the play!

Journeys Beyond the Sunset

On a boat made of ice cream,
We sailed through a bubble stream.
With fish wearing hats and shoes,
They danced to the colors of blues.

We met a cat with a guitar,
Singing songs sous le bazaar.
His whiskers twirled with delight,
As he strummed through the night.

The stars winked in a soft haze,
While dolphins joined in the praise.
They flipped and splashed with great cheer,
As we laughed and drank ginger beer.

At the end of the day's run,
We found a sun made of fun.
It melted all worries away,
As we danced till the break of day.

Secrets Written in the Tides

The waves whispered tales on the shore,
Of a crab who dreamed to explore.
With a map drawn in yellow sand,
He plotted his trip to a far-off land.

A parrot squawked, "Don't be a fool!
Stay here and learn the sea's cool rule."
But off went the crab in a flash,
Past seashells, and each wayward splash.

He met a turtle playing chess,
In a shell of an old red dress.
"Your life is but a game," she said,
"Just don't lose your shell or dread."

When the tide turned, he lost his way,
In a whirl of fish that went astray.
But the laughter echoed through the night,
As he danced with stars, oh what a sight!

Paintings on a Sea-Salted Canvas

The beach was a splash of colors bright,
With squirt-gun battles, oh what a sight.
Canvas of jelly and ocean spray,
As seagulls laughed and flew away.

A painter in flip-flops sat near,
With an easel made of crabs and cheer.
He painted clouds shaped like snacks,
While fishy friends kept counting stacks.

Amid the brush strokes so free,
A group of clams threw a tea party.
They served cookies with a funny twist,
A treat that no one could resist.

With laughter beneath the sun's ray,
Each splash turned brighter in playful sway.
And as the day faded to night,
The canvas glowed, a laughter light.

In the Heart of the Leafy Labyrinth

In a maze of leaves, we played tag,
With squirrels wearing a fashionable rag.
They giggled and swung from the trees,
While bees buzzed songs in the breeze.

A raccoon claimed he was the king,
Ordered nuts and danced like a fling.
He wore a crown made of old floss,
And laughed at the thought of being boss.

The shadows grew long, turned to fun,
As we chased fireflies, one by one.
Each flicker held a giggling sprite,
Who whispered secrets of the night.

In this labyrinth where laughter spun,
We found magic that couldn't be done.
With every twist, a new delight,
In leafy wonders under the moonlight.

Whispers of the Emerald Canopy

In the jungle where the parrots squawk,
Old monkeys gossip and love to talk.
They tell of fruits that wiggle and jiggle,
Like jelly on a plate, oh what a giggle!

A sloth hangs low, he's lost in a dream,
While ants parade in a silly team.
A toucan mocks with a vibrant beak,
Making faces, never feeling meek!

The iguanas strut, looking quite dapper,
In shades of green, they could win a capper.
Every rustle, oh, what a thrill!
In this leafy realm, laughter's the drill!

When rain begins to pour, they all flee,
With slips and trips, oh, so carefree.
Dancing in puddles, oh what a sight!
In the emerald canopy, joy takes flight!

Shadows on the Sunlit Shore

On sandy banks where crabs scurry fast,
Shells drop and tumble, oh what a blast!
Seagulls squawk with a great big grin,
Playing tag with the waves, let the fun begin!

A flip-flop's lost, the tide claims its prize,
While sunburnt tourists roll their eyes.
Beach balls bounce, oh what a fiasco,
Kids chasing shadows as the sun starts to go!

The octopus waves from beneath the foam,
While starfish gather, plotting their home.
Sandcastles giggle, their towers all lean,
As a wayward dog gives them a clean sheen!

With cocktails flailing, umbrellas in tow,
The beach party rages, the laughter does flow.
Under the sun, with mischief galore,
Shadows dance on this sunlit shore!

The Hidden Lagoon's Sonnet

In a lagoon where the frogs croak loud,
A fish in a hat swims past the crowd.
He quips and quicks with a wiggle and splash,
As turtles chuckle, making a bash!

Lily pads bounce, like beds of delight,
While dragonflies flirt, in a fluttering flight.
The water a mirror, reflecting a grin,
As the breeze carries secrets with a whimsical spin!

A crab with a shell that's sparkly bright,
Takes waves on the chin, with pure delight.
With friends all around in this watery nest,
Every croak and splash is a playful jest!

As night falls gently, the stars glisten,
In our hidden lagoon, hear the critters listen.
With laughter and joy, a festive encore,
A sonnet of secrets, forever more!

Dance of the Coconut Palms

Underneath the palms, where the breezes play,
Coconuts juggle, they're here to stay!
They tumble and roll with a bump and a thump,
While the monkeys all cheer, doing the clump!

With every sway, there's a coconut show,
The crabs do the salsa, oh what a glow!
Grasshoppers hop to the rhythm in tune,
As fireflies twinkle beneath the moon!

In this palm grove, with laughter so bright,
The breeze carries giggles into the night.
With nutty confetti swirling around,
The dance of the palms, pure joy is found!

So if you hear laughter and see a parade,
Join in the festivity, don't be afraid.
For in this palm world, fun knows no bounds,
Where coconuts groove and happiness sounds!

The Call of the Wild

In the jungle where the parrots squawk,
A monkey steals a coconut and tries to talk.
The toucans laugh with their beaks so bright,
As the sloth waves slowly, saying, "What a sight!"

The vines hang low, tangled like my hair,
An iguana sunbathes without a care.
While a spider spins a web of silly dreams,
The capybara just giggles, or so it seems.

Dancing feet on a ground of squishy moss,
Everyone's invited, there's never a loss.
The rhythm of the leaves calls out for fun,
Join the wild parade before the day is done!

So grab your hat and slip on your shoes,
In this vibrant place, there's never to lose.
We'll jump over puddles and climb a tall tree,
In this crazy haven, life's as bright as can be!

Untamed

A parrot with a bow tie struts around,
While a loud frog sings, never out of sound.
The monkey moonwalks on a branch so thin,
Cheering on the raccoon with her shiny tin.

Bamboo sticks dancing in the breezy air,
Where toucans gossip without a single care.
A sloth slow-dances, taking his sweet time,
While the tortoise plays maracas, feeling sublime.

Laughter echoes from each leafy nook,
With a secret party in a storybook.
Fireflies flicker like jazz hands in flight,
As the stars above join in the delight.

Come join the chaos, leave worries behind,
In this land where fun is the only kind.
With a wink and a grin, let's take a chance,
In the wild where all the creatures dance!

Islanders' Chorus at Dusk

As the sun dips low, the crickets start to sing,
A crab with sunglasses waltzes, what a thing!
The coconuts shake on the palm tree tall,
While the playful sea turtles begin to sprawl.

Bright hues fill the sky, the colors collide,
With laughter and joy, they let the night slide.
A dolphin leaps high, showing off his flair,
As the curious fish gather, dancing everywhere.

The sand tickles toes as shadows take flight,
With the rumble of waves, we party all night.
The stars twinkle brightly, like confetti from space,
In this island world, we've found our place.

So grab a shell, let's shout and cheer,
These fun-loving critters all swing near.
We'll serenade the ocean, our tunes set free,
In this merry place, just you and me!

Echoes of Rainforest Enchantment

Amidst the trees where the wild things play,
A jaguar prances, flaunting his sway.
The mushrooms giggle, growing all around,
As the snake tells tales of treasures he found.

With the echo of laughter through misty air,
A tapir dances, full of bold flair.
Birds of vivid colors join in the fun,
As the day starts fading, and night has begun.

Banana peels slide underfoot here,
As the chattering monkeys bring everyone cheer.
With a cauldron of smiles in this lush retreat,
We create our own rhythm, skipping to the beat.

Let's gather 'round and hear the tales retold,
Where wild creatures share secrets of gold.
In this leafy wonderland, spirits stay free,
In the laughter of the wild, you'll find glee!

Pulses of Serenity in Paradise

Gentle waves crash on a vibrant shore,
As the seagulls roam and the crabs explore.
A palm tree sways with a twist and a shout,
While the starfish lounge, giving the sun a clout.

With hammocks strung, dreams dance in the breeze,
While lizards recline with the utmost ease.
A piña colada cheers, with flavors so bright,
As all the beach bunnies hop into the night.

The rhythm of the waves plays a sweet tune,
With fireflies flickering under the moon.
While fish join in with their shimmering scales,
Making this paradise where laughter prevails.

So gather around, let's toast to our luck,
In this charming spot, where we truly struck.
With joy in our hearts, under the sky's vast blue,
In this lovely haven, fun always ensues!

Landscapes of Unspoken Love

In the heat where laughter blooms,
A coconut whispers, mischief looms.
Tanned skins race on golden shores,
Love's a game; who keeps the score?

Beneath the palms, a dance so sly,
A seagull swoops, oh my, oh my!
With every splash, hearts skip and glide,
These stolen glances, we can't hide.

Limes roll loose from sailor's hands,
As cheeky breezes lift our plans.
Two sunburns that mirror each fate,
Who knew love could be such a state?

Wrapped in towels, after sunburn's bite,
We laugh at crabs scuttling in flight.
In every giggle, a promise rings,
For love that's woven in silly things.

The Alchemy of Ocean Dreams

In a world where fishwear shoes,
And mermaids giggle at human blues.
The waves concoct a potion sweet,
With every splash, the secrets greet.

Octopuses trade their pearls for smiles,
While dolphins juggle for a while.
We sip on drinks with a twist of fun,
In a land where time's eternally spun.

One folk tale glows beneath the moon,
When sea turtles dance to a reggae tune.
Laughter bubbles up like foam,
When even the seashells feel at home.

Caught in a net of sandy cheer,
A treasure chest of whimsy near.
The ocean hums a playful rhyme,
Where dreams float gently, free of time.

Jewels of the Forgotten Bay

Underneath the sand lies glee,
The crabs tell tales, come listen, see!
Coconuts roll like treasure chests,
With giggles trapped in sun-kissed quests.

Fishermen steal starlight from skies,
As seagulls plot with glinting eyes.
A splash from dolphins' playful flips,
Turns shy whispers to playful quips.

In rusty boats, old tales delight,
Of jellies dancing, carefree night.
Forgotten gems in sunset's haze,
They dazzle bright in playful ways.

Under waves where laughter stays,
The ocean sparkles through the craze.
Amongst the shells, love's laughter plays,
In the bay where joy always sways.

Safari for the Soul

In the jungle, monkeys sass,
Swinging low and stealing grass.
With every swing, they tease and cheer,
Making sure that fun is near.

On a path with laughter loud,
Baboons strut, as though they're proud.
Chasing butterflies, we stomp our feet,
In this wild dance, we can't be beat.

Lions snore, but dreams will soar,
As parakeets gossip, around we explore.
Life's a zoo of laugh and play,
In sunny shores where we roam each day.

With every step, joy's the goal,
In a crazy ride, we find our role.
In the heart of wild, a secret cool,
The best adventure? It's the thrill of the fool.

The Folklore of Frangipani

In gardens where the flowers smile,
Frangipani dances, all the while.
Whispers of bees in a buzzing spree,
Tell tales of love, as sweet as can be.

A squirrel in shades, playing hide and seek,
Dreams of the world from its cozy peak.
It finds a crown in a petal's embrace,
Claiming the throne in this flowered space.

Then there's that lizard, sly and spry,
Who thinks he's the king, oh my, oh my!
He raises his tail, does a silly jig,
Pretending he's grand with a dance so big.

And if you listen, with ears that are keen,
You'll catch the vibrations of laughter unseen.
In this garden lush, every creature agrees,
Life is a riot, with giggles like bees.

Murmurs from the Mangrove Mysteries

In the mangroves where the waters sway,
A crab tells jokes in a cheeky way.
He pinches with glee, while the fish just giggle,
As they wiggle and splash in a slippery wiggle.

The heron struts, with feathers so fine,
He thinks he's a runway model, divine.
But step too close, and he'll take flight,
Leaving behind a tail feather of fright.

And what of the turtle, slow but wise?
He tells of the stars disguised in the skies.
While munching on kelp, he'll softly croon,
About moonlit dances to a merry tune.

Underneath it all, the secrets unfold,
In whispers and chuckles, both daring and bold.
The mangrove reveals with a winking cheer,
The mysteries hidden, so close yet so dear.

Castaway Dreams Under Coconut Skies

On a beach where the coconuts fall,
A castaway dreams of a grand coconut ball.
With shells as drums, they'll dance all night,
While crabs play the flute, what a hilarious sight!

The palm trees sway, wearing hats made of leaves,
As the sands bring laughter, no one believes.
Oh, the seagulls screech, taking the stage,
Singing songs of mischief, acting their age.

A parrot named Pete, with colors so bright,
Tells funny tales until the moonlight.
He swoops and he dives, with a wink and a flair,
Dropping some gossip, oh what a dare!

So raise your coconuts, give a cheer!
For castaway dreams are nothing but dear.
With every wave, more smiles we find,
In this realm of joy, we're all so aligned.

Lost in the Labyrinth of Lush Green

In the maze of green, where shadows play,
A monkey swings in a cheeky ballet.
He loops and he twirls, shouting 'Catch me if you can!'
While the parrots hoot, 'What a clever plan!'

A frog in a puddle puts on a show,
Jumps like a dancer in flashy toe-to-toe.
He croaks with delight, feeling quite grand,
As grasshoppers clap, forming a band.

But the strangest of sights is a sloth up a tree,
Snoozing away, oh how funny to see!
He dreams of adventures, of food and of fun,
While the world below races, but he's never done.

In this labyrinth lush, we laugh and we roam,
Where every twist and turn feels like home.
Embracing the silly, the wild, and the keen,
Lost in the joy, in all of this green.

www.ingramcontent.com/pod-product-compliance
Lightning Source LLC
Chambersburg PA
CBHW072117070526
44585CB00016B/1481